The Lost Brother Alphabet

Kathy Engel

Copyright © 2020 by Kathy Engel

All rights reserved. No part of this book may be reproduced in any manner without written consent except for the quotation of short passages used inside of an article, criticism, or review.

Get Fresh Books, A Non-Profit Corporation
PO Box 901
Union, New Jersey 07083

gfbpublishing.org

ISBN: 978-1-7345802-1-1
Library of Congress Control Number: email info@gfbpublishing.org

Cover image: Philippe Cheng
Cover design: Roberto Garcia and Ann Davenport
Book design: Ann Davenport

The Lost Brother Alphabet

Kathy Engel

What we feel most has no name but amber, archers, cinnamon, horses and birds ...
—Jack Gilbert, "The Forgotten Dialect of the Heart"

... willingness to listen and to say all that we know, and feel—all that we dare—perhaps that will help us to build something better than we can even, now, imagine ...
—June Jordan, "Letter To My Friend"

For my partner in life, Jon

For my mother, Tinka

In memory: Herman Jay Engel   Timothy Jay Engel

1/5/20:
I asked [my mother]: *is it ok for you that I write about these things?*
She said: *if it helps someone...*

Contents

the body i write for	1
Horses, still	7
To Mourn the Living	8
A	10
Dad, Pete & Obama	11
The Beginning of the Alphabet	12
B (Best)	13
Block Island Tanka Morning	14
Annus Mirabilis	15
Begin again	16
B	17
Staying in My Dead Dad's Apartment	18
F	19
F (59)	20
Instructions to My Father on What Would Have Been Your 86th Birthday	21
G	22
Horse & Fire Dream	23
not there	24
I	25
Anniversary	26
Advice	27
Marlene's Dream	28
K	31
Coffee	32
L	35
I Stop for Beauty	36
M (Male)	37
I've known horses	38
Reading to the Dead	39
Text message from best friend in Buffalo	40
Father Tanka	41
M (Middle)	42
My daughter's convinced	43

To Kneel	44
Where	46
S & T	51
Stolen Grief	52
Haiku: Two Old Friends Meet in Agnostic Heaven	54
O	55
Praise Song for a Farmer	56
Eighty-Five	58
P	59
R	60
R (Remember)	61
Now I Pray	62
Breasts & Interrogation	64
More S	65
We Have Been Here a Long Time	66
T	67
Volunteer	68
W (Wrong)	69
Return	70
W	71
Y	72
Since We're Talking About Love	73
Amends to Parts of the Body	74
My father	76
Becoming	77
Gratitude	78
The Last Letter	79
Notes	81
Thank You	82
Acknowledgments	85
About the Poet	87

j

M   h

                          Z
          i

e   t

                k
    W   B

                A

the body i write for

        is singular & plural, wants to watch a whale for hours

          without reason, slick mysterious blueblack rise

            & drop, listen to its lone eternal horn,

                haunting ocean archive

            the smooth tan skin of crepe myrtle

        barely alive after first wind, blooms now,

      cone-shaped lanterns of crinkly pink or white petals

    dangling from antlers of bark, rooted near enough

  snowbell, kousa dogwood & mimosa to share

a village of mycelium

    the body is daughter & mother, lover & lover,

        wave & particle, track & train hovering around the bend with its death eye,

          long moan & grammar of loss she talks to tolstoy's anna:

            don't leap she calls back into the story: *love yourself more than vanquished*
                desire for a man, pride having broken his horse's back beneath him

the child body traveled by train at babylon the wheels wrote she rode a metaphor of missing

dear cheryl, thank you for asking me to write who is the body i write for

is this zuihitsu? i'm trying to fit

into the name of something

i'm learning to write for the decimated bodies offered again & again by feline cohabitants

mouse haunch, rabbit leg, pierced vole, knowing it is loyalty that brings these body parts

still i battle squeamishness & the limitations of a gentrified, bifurcated mind

is the body the one writing or the body written for or to, or does it matter?

the body is indebted to generations of bodies whose names i haven't learned, embracing a

multitude of languages & places,

often afraid to leave home

the writing body knows she must write the body more honestly the white she lives is not a true color, but its weight is undeniable and if not interrupted will continue to kill

the inaccuracy of how light moves

the inaccuracy of scale

the inaccuracy of a body

        to know another body

        the inaccuracy of love

the body is in the end   itself

                        craving redemption

j

M   h

                        z
        i

e   t

            W   k
                              B

                    A

Horses, still

One chilly April midnight when I was ten
the farmer in my life woke me in flannel
nightgown & sleepy feet to pad down
the dirt trail, white mare heaving on yellow
straw This is the story I keep telling;
we all have one Who was birthed that
night became my hooved companion,
quieted my train-track heart torn between
locations & parents—Jewish girl with
a braid & Arab horse with high flicking
tail weren't meant to be together or leap
over fences so we flew into our own animal
grammar until I left to be grown—equine
murmur not tough enough to prove my worth
Today I reject harness, steel bit—the gate opens

To Mourn the Living

This is the husk of shared cells
This is the stray word untranslated
This is the testament of not knowing
This is the page of forgetting
This is the shard of remembering
This is the invisible map of animal
This is humor buried like a bone
This is the raspy girl & ponytail
This is the long stride & cigarette
This is the mystery of a few years older
This is the sister   This is the brother
This is the tender carrying on shoulders to touchdown
This is the looking up while crossing the street
This is the looking up
This is a sports car & basketball
This is a dude ranch & book chapters
This is a broken kidney
This is whiskey & cocaine
& this is the jabberwocky
No, this is the jackhammer
              No this is the misty tale
                    No this is the turning away
This is the un named name of dis ease
This is the hem of need & the pus of shame
This is the pulse ramshackled
This is the white pill, the unmarked bottle & saliva
This is the lie, this is how it masquerades as love
This is the shadow
This is the next lie
This is the stone of estrangement
This is the wilt & axe
This has no color
This has no taste
This voice has unlearned itself
This is not spoken

This is the body breaking as it tells
This is the harness of the throat
This is the scorch of letting go
This is the rot of not believing
This is the rancid pulp of regret
This is dream attempting to mend like a weaver
This is how the eyes hold their water
This is the residue of softness clamoring
This is where I go when I'm lost

A

again
the horse leads me
to water,
she steps over stones
like a ballerina,
breathes hot air into
my waiting face,
she stomps, curls her
brown slender leg,
scuffs the ground
with striped hoof
the way I want to;
instinctively I look
for you, brother
who led us both,
girl & horse, brown
hair swishing, lead shank
in one hand, coca-cola
in the other, only a rifle
then, for duck hunting;
he's gone, I say
over & over, aloud;
the horse throws her head
back, leads me,
again, to water

Dad, Pete & Obama

When Pete sang at the Lincoln Memorial I called to ash
I had played Pete as your last breath slipped out,
the rest of you already gone
Pete ushered you; your hero sang for the man
whose name you spoke the week you died:
Obama, you said, sipping water, *I believe something is happening,
don't you?* Pete, with his grandson who lived in Nicaragua, the country
we loved in its burning birth, Pete who wouldn't testify, Pete Civil Rights,
Pete Peace, Pete 1199, Pete this land—Pete Clearwater, Pete
& Toshi, Pete & Brother Kirkpatrick, Pete &
June reading poems at the UN rally circa 1983, Pete the unwavering
for all who were taken, all who picketed & as Pete said:
for the young people who taught us not to be afraid those Montgomery
sit-in days, Pete in his power, in the place of power,
suspenders & banjo, train chug of workers
belting out a new old gusty day, ghosts of resistance swaying
past the monument, feeding the hungry crowd, this day when Pete sang
at the Lincoln Memorial I called to you
who took a bus alone to DC at 80 to protest:
I called to your ash, Dad, who took me there first

The Beginning of the Alphabet

Ahhhhh They say the

stomach is the real

heart I run to the toilet

Anger   Apology

I am so sorry so sorry sorry   I

Am

sorry so sorry

Addiction   Absolution?

                                                        Almost

Always   Away

(the A in that Ache)

B (Best)

Brother, you were to me
Then
Your long arms ready

Block Island Tanka Morning

Windmill tilts me sun
mill melts me cormorant talks
to me mourning dove
souls me church bell confuses
me grass grows inside me

Annus Mirabilis

Passover, I miss my father, horse
radish, salt water, Elijah's chair
& a cracked door carving

modern air We used to scan
the holy book, revise as though
we could delete the notion

of the *chosen*! This first night
of passing over in a year of
wonders, for my father who art

in heaven I read ancient
Hebrew Muslim verse I can't
pronounce & lift my glass

Begin again

said the cardinal
in his redness
to my window
Begin again
said the moth
invading rice
Begin again
the earth admonished

B

You loved that smothered buttered bread
We called you Bimbo after the song, blonde then, blue-eyed boy: *Bimbo*
Bimbo where you gonna go e o ... does your mother know ...

Each year your bad valve kidney probed, poked,
tube through penis, hospital after hospital, bleeding,
parents combing the country for the best

In Boston Children's, surgery at 15, long handsome hair, flirting
with nurses, there was a girl, her whole body burned, sitting gauzed
in a chair; did it break you?

Staying in My Dead Dad's Apartment

I blew a fuse trying to heat up the bathroom for my daughter
had to call Manny the Super on Sunday night during
Yankees game—he panted up last flight of stairs—I thought
I might be responsible for heart failure & dragon landlady
would discover I was squatting in apartment ignorant of trip switches
I opened the window to check the weather—it wouldn't close again—
found some of Dad's d-200 or whatever that can is in a corner,
sprayed it like crazy, stood there sweating, afraid to open
the window, unexpected October sun leaking through the skylight
I cracked the chemex coffee pot, one of three, different sizes on a light wood
shelf Dad made, returned it to the shelf with a sticky note: *broken,
will replace, k.e.*
I bumped into my dad in the narrow kitchen where he used to stand, his blue
& white striped shredding terry bathrobe half open, talking in early
morning, concocting his "sugar omelet" with berries—
he said: *Don't worry about it, Kath, these are just things* We had a cup
of coffee; he gave an odd disappearing smile then went back to death

F

All happy families are alike. Each unhappy family is unhappy in its own way.
—Leo Tolstoy, *Anna Karenina*

Tolstoy got it wrong
What is a happy family?
Today's lesson: F

Brother as friend?
Fiend?

You forgot to leave my dream
Just walked in last night
like a cowboy

Then fled again
I fortify, fortify

F (59)

you were, must have
stowed forty designer
ties in your angry closet—
the only fabric left
unraveling; you even
took the threads

Instructions to My Father on What Would Have Been Your 86th Birthday

1.

Let Id & Super Ego waltz like Fred & Ginger
or tumble forward, huffing & puffing,
one behind the other, Piglet & Pooh
Or let them fight

2.

Come back into our house near the sea
where you sat frozen just after we moved,
staring at the high-arched windows Now
open your arms & bless us

3.

Forgive your mother for needing
you too much, my mother for
not needing you, me for
growing Forgive yourself

4.

Make that film The one in which
you are the protagonist, free to
fail Don't splice the bad
parts Sail

G

Good
or not good

Hand at groin
on the couch after dinner

Grandiose, a
gazillion everythings

Grief is a body part
Gone, brother,

gone
But a gun

Horse & Fire Dream

I race this frenzied mare
night after fire night; she chases
her foal, its scant fetlocks

singed, thin wavering
whinny Who holds the reins?
Did war never end? Did marching

in circles dizzy me? Who did
my good life incarcerate? Did
my daughters get

lost? What is lost? How much time
left to perform memory
transfusion? The metaphor

walks, twists Perjurious
I kick this dream over
like a kerosene can,

galloping flame I reach
for medicine, sleepless mare

not there

i am not there i ask permission for the way to grieve forgiveness for my distance my comfort i am not there i look for meaning even blame as i go about my life eating laughing bathing filling my car with gas going to work i am not there this is not metaphor i want to be useful i am secretly relieved & guilty it is not me my family but any day it could be it is someone i know today yesterday i can't name the feeling of not being there in the horror i count who i know is there i count each day & insist i will not stop counting but the distance like a drawbridge will open out over time & memory will blur another thing will happen near or far i am not there i want to be loyal to the pain i want to be responsible i want the best of what is human in me to bloom like a parachute & make me powerful i still want to sleep & laugh & live i am not there i want to roll back time & wake up from a nightmare i can't explain but i can i want to be useful i want to be good i want to define natural disaster & imperial power i am not there i want to know who's right i want to write it so beautifully so poignantly as if never said before i want to conjure simile to construct diction & syntax shake the world into healing with the form of my lyric i want to invent empathy & rebuild homes i am not there i want to bring life back honor color joy & resistance in the respectful way i don't want to be morose i am not there i want to do the right thing i want to go there i don't know if that will be useful or just make me feel like it is i can't say i don't know how to measure perspective i don't know i'm not there i walk around in my town with replaceable equipment i don't know what to do i don't know how to think i don't know what language to pray which deity would allow such relentless assault i don't know how to act or what to make i am pathetic i itch inside the smallness of my abilities i scratch at the failure in my throat I'm not there & don't trust myself to tell the truth this is not a poem

I

Inside
your insatiable
inside your instant
gratification   inside
your chocolate yodels
inside your irritated
knee   your itching sex
your illicit   inside inside
inside the ink of you
the I of you   the irrepressible
innermost   inside there

would you were invincible
would you imagined
the possible   the everyday
not inured   not invaded
irreconcilable   was it
involuntary   inside
the I of you   inside

Anniversary

Honor the day the horse legged out
Honor her warm puffs of breath,
whisker threads Honor the re-
telling, equine dust, fresh-cut
grass, blood in straw, her slow
death years later after un-birth,
limp foal pulled from inside
like a bad tooth, body heavy
with ache; honor the waiting
for death, the unsaid infection,
honor the drunk farmer who
was also a father and let her
free in the field with stallion—
can a horse be raped?
Honor the girl who leaned into
the warm fur neck of the four legged
& the farmer planting the tree
together in silence after lifting
the weight of a life, how they dug
a deep bed in the soil, laid down a
hooved body; honor green apples
when they pop out of buds like small
bullets; honor drip of verse incessant
as a busted faucet, what a girl, then
a young woman learns about birth
or death, any uncovering, who
becomes a mother, tells her daughters
the story, siphoning out the gin
in a coke can; honor the daughters
who find fallen apples, bruising
as they land, family myth cracking
like a dead branch—the truth—still
a man and a child picking through
leaves, finding their way, daily

Advice

*I have a headache and my ear hurts
from writing about dead dads,* I tell my
daughter, 17, as we lounge across
her bed Almond eyes askance, her lip
curves just a bit—*Don't be a tortured
poet; write about something else,* she chides
Ok, I skirt, *I'll try; I'm also tired
of writing about war* Without a blink
she says once more, *Not a tortured poet,
Mom,* perfect oval face, auburn hair
flashing *Right,* I say

Marlene's Dream

My sister's friend Marlene
dreams about me:
In a garage writing a book I chalked on a wall:
Does Stegner read Babar? Does Babar read Stegner?
Who is Wallace Stegner & why
don't I know his work? I spent
many hours with Babar, however:
he holds the secret of memory in
his young gray trunk & he lisps
I know he's afraid of Rataxes
the rhino, not sure he has a sense
of humor I think he's confused
about empire & can't leave
Celeste Why was I in a garage?
Am I a car, a broken carburetor,
merely a clutch? Are my brakes
wet? & why is Marlene, who
charts children's minds, along
with my sister, dreaming about me?
Is my sister Stegner & I'm Babar?
Then who is Marlene? Is she
afraid I've parked in my sister's
garage? At least I'm grateful
to her that I'm writing a book
& I know what to do with a wall

j

h

M

z

i

e   t

W   k

                        B

A

K

My letter, can I keep it?
Kite stuck in tree remember
when you stuck gum in my hair

My kids remember
your big lipped loud
juicy kisses

Kiss what's gone
Kiss the sad kidney
Kiss the pain
     Don't explain

Kiss kill killed yourself how could you

Coffee

Hand-rubbed dark
oil: I share my
addiction with
the loved
dead My coffee-
berry meets me
in a favorite
ample vessel—
announcing where
I've been or hope
to go: Buffalo,
Bolivia, Kenya

My father poured
my first cup when
I was eight, glint
in his eye, defying
Mrs. Renkins, third
grade teacher who
insisted it would
stunt my growth
He penned a caffeine
verse his last years,
sent me Bach's *Coffee
Cantata* in duplicate

Balzac died
of it: flood
of bloodied mahogany
ink burst vein to
page I dream
a *Coffee Anthology*—
unfiltered, musky
Mahmoud Darwish
measured his

exactly each Beirut
morning, 1982,
bombs exploding,
beloved steaming pot
of thick black

In Grace's 11th Street
kitchen long-haired
women mapped out
sit-ins, peace & PTA—
pencils & newspapers
piling up, old-fashioned
New York coffee time

D from the island
Grenada roasts his
in the next town B
of Shinnecock Nation
names her smoky brew
Native Coffee

My father gulped his
after toast with jam,
& on the weekends,
pancakes, nuts he
mashed in a mortar
and corn flour

No electric pot for him
He ground a mean bean,
boiled water in a kettle,
early—old
bathrobe & slippers,
long talks at the table

Where did my coffee-loving father go?

My grandmother, Henrietta,

savored hers for hours,
porcelain cup & saucer,
large hands sifting
& folding her
famous buttery
plum cake—Henry
Street to 63rd, granules
of her transplanted
voice, like sugar, or
Yiddish Like loss

Java grounds & ash
help Russian kale grow
Before morning compost spread,
Jon brings the first cup
to me, early, in bed

L

The letters you left
I never saw them
Your wife told me
I would never want to
You who loved language,
let it be your last lick,
show your last loss like
a bad card hand This
was not leverage The
letters, last lords of pain
Did she burn them
What did the police
do with them   Lift the
legs from their bodies,
leave them to languish,
last testaments

Not least I love your
laugh, head tilted back,
full body When did that
tumble laugh go like
the leaves shaking down
the maple outside
my lonesome window

I Stop for Beauty

At Grace Church, drawn
to go in, more to stand in
sapphire dusk of worship,
familiar corner of my city
I stay outside, stare at
the stone structure, angled
as a Giacometti face What
is *real,* whose God is in there,
blue as the day life started?
On the sidewalk I'm transfixed,
the cobalt of memory cloaks
me, fatherless mother
of grown women, aging daughter,
the wings of me flying
& staying, always both,
as the hem of day meets night
& I'm learning to breathe,
cement under my feet This
is where my father stood, where
he stooped down to hold
my daughter's fine-boned hand

M (Male)

We used to sit in a big chair near
the tub, sisters—Mom in bubbles,
a wet washcloth over her bosom,
not for cover, but heat We dipped
her creams, giggled in steam

What did you do then, only boy,
as secrets passed through water,
naked   Were you hunting with
your stepfather, combing comics,
smoking Marlboros, as we
sequestered, cooing,
ache brewing

I've known horses

bay, chestnut, Appaloosa & rank as whiskey at the White
Horse Tavern on Hudson

I've watched a skinny lone colt trot through Managua's
unmarked streets in wartime

I've dodged the hooves of shaggy Clydesdales, spurred into frenzy
by police at a sit-in

But the horses I've known—all night in the hot furred air
of becoming Then the laying

back into the earth Their ancient ink eyes see to the side;
their ghosts gallop at my shore

Reading to the Dead

I talk to Dad when I'm driving,
hand poised to call, against
the law, to give him the latest
Taha Muhammad Ali has died,
I tell him, as if to say: *he is joining*
you, Dad, with his strong nose &
half smile—the Palestinian poet
who recited at his street corner
store for the only reliable
critics, a story for a tchotchke
So I read Taha to Dad when I'm
off the expressway & back roads,
in bed with a glass of red wine, staring
out the window at death's truth
as dusk hits like a target
just as he read me Yeats before I knew
the trees were in their autumn beauty

Text message from best friend in Buffalo

off the coast of Florida a beached mother whale [died]
and the calf will be euthanized
what have we
done

we off
we coast
we beach
we mother
we whale
we [died]
we calf
we will
we be
we euthanize
we what
we have
we done

Father Tanka

Years since I read you
Spring and Fall: To a Young Child
sitting on the side
of your bed, blanched eyelids, face
edged as a ski, sad mountain

M (Middle)

Child
I am no longer
You force me older
You shrank
Even those muscles
Then air
Now my big brother, not here
For so long, not there/for me

My daughter's convinced

the end of the world is this day Or the very next
With each wind shock or quick dark she makes her
pronouncement The God of unforgiveness has
finally arrived I might suggest each 24

hours are *a miracle of light, the coil of a new
beginning* But I say nothing: count my dead
friends & family That's what a parent does:
lie about the end of the world & death

To Kneel

The black men who make wages
from the brutal banging of the skull,
pounding of the knees, arms
reaching like branches in the long
arc of a pass, now kneel
The muscles of their souls,
the soles of their cleats, stretch
of their thighs speak Fans & refs
yell, commentators jabber & behold:
one knee, hand to ground,

they kneel, the weight
of their built-up bodies
pulled earthward as if called
by those from before
to kneel *now*, refusing to salute
this country's killing field
Those with the heart to be the lonely
first; *their* knees sing Jobs at stake,
they kneel for the inheritors For the future
dignity of bodies to choose to stand

or touch down & the joining, too—
some, then flocks, arms threaded,
waving flags of jersey-ed bodies,
an anthem, for the uncountable—
to be counted & to those
who drop to the knee
only in the recesses of a locked
back room or those who switch & bait
in the light, amid the throngs—or those
who hide behind their whiteness—

who will be there to kneel for you
when such a time comes, as it ***will***

come? What will you say when
your children or your grandchildren,
their friends or lovers ask
what parts of your bodies
touched the ground
in the moment of loyalty,
or the moment of betrayal?
What would I?

Where

The message comes through aol.com, finds me off
balance in a small school in Jersey, snow
puffing down, no newspaper in sight
Hi love, the message reads, *thinking of you
in London, heart in Gaza*
Unsigned, I know the e-mail address like my own
name, reply too quickly, no words in the text, then
correct my mistake, *love,* I write, *yes,
heart in Gaza* I don't know
what else to say

*

Is there a poem in Gaza that hasn't been written

*

I know you're Palestinian, he said to me, *I know you are,*
a man in the Dheisheh camp

Guards questioned me at the Tel Aviv airport:
where did we go, did we visit a mosque, a synagogue

Did I eat the poems of Darwish,
drink coffee he brewed, each grain an oud

standing at his window of fire,
my tax dollars shining through?

In my suitcase I wrapped
shards of a bulldozed home, the only teacup,

flew back, a dirty gull with a passport,
each story contraband

We are related, I rub olive oil on arms, belly, neck, soak bread in it—
I had to see for myself, after Seder's bitter herbs,

taste the lie
Now I understand, my mother said, *now I understand,*

reading my journey, Jewish girl, promised land, betrayal,
a poem in Gaza

j

M   h

                          z
            i

e   t

          W   k
                                    B

                    A

S & T

We hold your suicide like broken glass,
each with our different fingers & cupped hands

One of us a braided girl sitting beside you on a horse trailer
ramp, laughing so hard she vomits on your shoulder

One of us wispy & story-filled, long cotton dress trailing
the grass, her nickname, a bird you call

One of us much younger, face open as a palm; you drive her anywhere
in your sports car, pack of cigarettes rolled in t-shirt sleeve,

countless girlfriends, whiskey, high school backgammon,
bad kidney & love of Faulkner

These holding fingers you slipped through again &
again after we grew, differently, into women and mothers

I would settle for *sentimental* in exchange for one true
sentence these last twenty years Your suicide,

Tim, is not glass or shard; our different shapes, your sisters,
not clear; we spill, slide & sit still You have killed

Stolen Grief

Thirty years ago my father
followed me south to a new
country made of old blood,

was gifted a wooden
rocker carefully packed
in twine, set it up on the hill

outside his homemade
Vermont cabin Today his
widow tells me she's sold

the cabin & the fields,
stored the chair in my
cousin's basement

I don't particularly
cherish things, but now
I search each light-

filled & shadowed
inch of my home for an
artifact—find photos,

an old terry robe &
a Gerard Manley Hopkins
book, its pages yellowed

by the imprint from
my father's deep-set eyes
That should be enough,

along with what really
counts, so why, as I
begin to imagine how

I will leave what I love
to those I love, am I
pierced by the image

of light-varnished wood,
a Nicaraguan chair
rocking in a basement

Haiku: Two Old Friends Meet in Agnostic Heaven

Chelsea to Thetford,
Tenth to Eleventh Streets, Dad
& Grace are talking

O

Or
Oxy
Or
Overdose before the gun
No one told us
We could have guessed
Pain makes a person old
Or
Oh no
O's in moon
The moan of distance looms
Voice turns to ice
O moon, o haunt of loon, o round:
You gave up on my brother (I did)

Praise Song for a Farmer

Dear God I never believed in,
praise the potato, praise Russet,
Katahdin, praise driving Geraldine
home who worked seasonally, praise
her pipe & the bad ones that got
tossed off the harvester, praise tacked-
up shack, praise her blackness,
praise train tracks, my whiteness,
bare legs dangling from the truck's
front seat, praise
our windowed ample home,
praise all things being unequal,
praise the farmer, my stepfather, who
spoke to no one more or less than
another, praise the frost when it
waits for harvest, praise
enduring when it doesn't, praise
sweet manure perfume, praise the
farmer's name for it & our kids
name for him: *Honey*—
praise dirt in the teeth,
praise bullshit,
praise mashed, boiled, baked,
sour cream & butter,
praise scalloped, fried & potato pancakes,
praise the horse's stomach that
can't upchuck, has to walk it off or
die, praise few words exact
as thorn, praise nicknaming neighbors
after animals, not the other way around,
praise sleepless potato price check,
price check, storm check,
hidden booze, praise Claribel
the angry Angus cow, motherhood
dried up too soon, praise the pigs

I fed birdseed, praise a phrase of soil
survives the glut: *for sale, for sale, for
sale,* praise red tractor, green pickup, a farmer's
lifted index finger, praise the potato, Russet,
Katahdin, praise back broken never
heals, praise aspirin, praise sandy salt
dunked starlit corn blackened husk
over fire, praise mucky pond & ocean mouth, each
burial site—dog, pony, donkey, goat,
& duck, praise duck blind at dawn, praise
nipping Blues, praise sailing on ice,
face cold cracked,
praise pumpkins bent by blight,
their orange punched-in skin
praise the potato—Russet, Katahdin,
Red Bliss Blue & Purple Yukon Gold Sweet
Round or Long White Fingerling, praise
the farmer, praise the farmer, praise
the farmer, praise the farm

Eighty-Five

My mother's alone in her house
as the storm turns the corner,
her husband's bear body
gone She gets smaller &
braver—daily walks,
legs that burst into blood

at the slightest brush against
skin & fear of dawn
I want to ask: *Mom, what
does it feel like each morning
to be this close to death,
so alive?*

Like the soft blanket on her soft
sofa, I want tenderness to cover
my filial annoyance at simply
being different—her quick
consonants neat as labeled folders,
my compass-less vowels, paper piles

Funny, my daughter smiles:
*you get upset when I say to you
the things you say to your mom*
Funny I want to be wise as
my daughter, to melt into speech
so my mother will know exactly

P

Pray for the story, all the parts
Pray for placenta
Pray for the boy & man promise
Pray for quick mind & agile legs pumping
Pray for the prologue
Pray for the lack of prophylaxis
Pray for how he was parent
Pray for the wild propeller of his parting
Pray for the children left to pay
Pray for their bloom and protection
    Pray for the blousy peony, the wilting plume
Pray for the wife who pardons
Pray for her torn proclamation
Pray for all who remain, their sticky paths
Pray for the pining
Pray for the prognosis & lack of prognosis
Pray for the lonely pit
Pray for his mother, her devastated progeny
Pray for his dead father, punctured pride
Pray for each sister, her pulse, her profusion
Pray for the brother he was, his profligacy
Pray for the body part—kidney, neck, knee, penis
Pray for proportion, & pray for lack of proportion
Pray for the past
    Pray for the qualifier & the unexpected pronoun
Pray for what is private
Pray for the possible
    Still pray for what is possible

R

When the reflexologist rubs
my feet, does she feel you, nerve
endings radiating, resisting peace?

It's all relative What is rhyme
or reason? I am your
relative; guilt, loss & rage

riddle my ribs This is real
Grief rides the rough-waved body
like a bucking horse I cling

to rhyme, confuse reason
Our sister & I rinse
with words, wrestle with rest,

watch for Mt. Rainier's snow-capped
cone to emerge, a sphinx over water,
as if reading tea leaves

I don't expect beauty or quiet
or even time to reveal your life
Or death

I'm not racing toward clarity
I ask for release
Remission

R (Remember)

when you repeated
such silly stuff
again & again
nonsense words like *lock ye do*
for *lock your door*?
I remember

Now I Pray

Ashen face, wool hat bobbing,
the young boy's eyes dart to me,
then up at the man pulling a roll-y
suitcase, whose hand he holds,
then back at me His legs move
as if without gravity The man asks:
do you know a church on this street
that serves free food? I want to say
I know That the names of churches
on an avenue called Americas roll
out of me I want to tell you
it is temporary, their condition:
suitcase, darting eyes, seeking free
food at 9 p.m. in a big city on a school night
I want to tell you I don't for a moment
wonder if that is really the boy's father
or uncle or legitimate caretaker—
something in the handholding &
eyes, having watched too many
episodes of *Law and Order* I want
to tell you I take them to a restaurant
& pay for a warm meal or empty
my wallet not worrying how
offensive that might be because
in the end hunger is hunger
I want to tell you I call someone
who loves them—that there is someone—
& say your guys are lost, can
you come? I want to tell you I sit
down on the sidewalk at the corner
of Waverly, & pray—that all
passing by, anonymous shoes
marking the pavement, join
in a chorus of prayer humming
like cicadas in the Delta I want to

tell you the boy & the man eat food
encircled by the warmth of bodies
I want to turn the cold night into a feast
I will tell you I am praying

Breasts & Interrogation

Even you, breasts that milk no more,
even if gush & cluck could come, the drops
would sour & curdle as I recall
the za'atar-haired mother from Lyd, ice packs
pressed on tender spouts to make her crack,
recording of a child's call shot
through the crusted wall into her prison cell

More S

Still, for you, I crave
some some some sweet
not shifty, not shut, not
shafted or shafting
That sea we soaked
I want to suck out
your shame, the sour,
the scary, the sold self,
salute your soul I am
your sister; here is my salt
Too late, this salve

We Have Been Here a Long Time

We sit on our bed, pens in hands, interspersing vowels
& *ah-ha*'s You read your *gratitudes* aloud: *Farmers, nurses*
The invisible world Me too Forty years, wars, & I can say,
me too We rename *failure*: *recovery*, our faces ravined, ruts
inside us Sunday morning sun streams through the window,
our winter skins We listen
to Eric Satie, Miles Davis I rename *recovery*: *evolution*
Humility Teach me music, I ask you after forty years
To ask, that's it—words naked, thirsty, newborn—
the long alone fight gives way like a violin string
if for a flash, an interlude
Fear, abandonment, you try the sounds
in your mouth We watch
the trees draw themselves in the sky, one sparrow
hopping *Intimacy,* a word that never paid rent
in your body before, you say slowly as if
discovering water, one drop, then another; a dash
of light settles on the quilt between us

T

Timothy, sweet hay
shares your name,
the photo of you
on Mom's piano,
lifting a bale,
looking over your tan
shoulder, flexed
honey hair

Volunteer

> *Volunteer: a plant that grows on its own without being seeded by a human*

Caw caw, finch talk, dewy haze & one pumpkin
appears, orange, ridge-skinned, out of compost,
leaning from its stem & then I see
another & another pop out, all leaning & full
Water splurges after a dry spell, & sprigs, called weeds,
poke up between Lavandula Provence & Siskiyou Pink
like new hair sprouts after a buzz cut
Running my path, I stop at the sight of a small buck
in a field Where did he come from,
his chandelier of antlers too heavy for his head?
I can smell the stillness he carries
in his tree of bone Geese honk as they
leave me for another season Who invited
any of us here Who gives permission to leave

W (Wrong)

wrong
when you are gone

your pain so plain & not
plain   & mine

what else to do
when we remain

wrong wrong wrong
so plain

I've made a poem of this pain
wrong wrong wrong

I search the ash, the stone, the flame
my own stain & yours

I need a window

Return

The animals camp out in the farm
of my body, a field of muscle, fat
& bone, sea of nerves; they mend
my vessels, sew back my arteries, sing
my stutter, gallop my missteps—first a
horse, then the others claim their places,
even snakes & insects swivel and swarm
I thought the rupture within was all
a human thing—the mother, the father,
the lost girl—now I understand, the earth
itself is calling & the animals, buried,
scattered, those who rise, snort, bellow,
murmur, hiss; their hooves, wings, fins
& tentacles seed the soil,
repair the soul

W

Wyoming,
the way rawhide scuffs
thighs, the way guys talk in a bunk
house & how it won't be your
life for real One star that
might have stayed in your face
when you laughed that way, roping
a calf, astride a roan mustang
galloping the plains, when life was still
stronger than the other Water bucket,
straw, how fingers grip wire &
the cutting Searing sun, night sliced
cool, sky wide as dream stretched over
dust & rock Then it was a woman,
her speckled green eyes, drops of
food in luscious hair & so you
came home For the woman For the
what? & it never felt like home
Not in Levi's or boots & so you
were lost Wyoming, woman, Wyandanch,
the town in your story, & I don't know
where, or when—why, just why

Y

This letter wants to say yes but like a rank horse it yanks to no
Year of no beginning, this lost letter only a *V* on a tree trunk
Yen for pickles in front of tv watching *I Spy*
Yell as your knee snaps out of itself on the field, me on your shoulders to touchdown
Yelp for your dog Puff named after the song, & the faraway land, Hona Lee
It's not about the yaw, or the Y chromosome
What yeast, what bread, what stirring
Yes, I give this letter to you who wanted to write All yours

Since We're Talking About Love

I will tell you that I used to lie down in a grassy field curved
into the belly of a bay horse with one white star on her broad face
calmed by warm breath sifting through whiskers onto my arm
& about love I can share with you that as a kid I had two friends
no one else could see named Wingding & Honey who traveled
frequently, & if a person inquired about their whereabouts,
I might've said, *Oh it's a big week for them, off to Switzerland,
then Japan for work*, but still scolded the waiter in the coffee shop
for failing to bring their fries Speaking of love, I should let you know
that I found some silvery cut hairs by the sink yesterday & ordinarily
I'd rant about the mess (who would leave cut hairs by the sink?!) but this time
swooped those silvery hairs & blew them into the air like eyelashes for luck
with the same lips that have been kissing the man who left the hairs for 44 years,
if you can believe it—& love being our subject I must reveal that despite
the shit-evil news of the conqueror, this very day I woke to a poem full
of kisses & licks, all of which is to say: poems of love, my friends,
fan open like peacock feathers & light the field of my morning

Amends to Parts of the Body

I'm sorry dear thighs for giving you a hard time,
I know you've just been doing your job, not
dwelling on size Why would I drag you down
when you carry me on, two steady trucks?

Stomach, oh soft heart in the middle
of the torso, how I have wronged you—
dark grounds of java at all hours, worry
turning & twisting where breath should thrive

Wrists, thick boats on masts, you flex, you hold,
anchor these hands like spools Have I ignored
the jut of you, the carve of you, lynchpin of
work, station for arm, with inadequate garnish?

Puffs around the mouth, I've done you wrong,
survived through generations of smile, you've
pressed through sadness, out of quivering lines—
please forgive my vanity, wishing you gone

Tongue, I tried to hide you, thought you
hideous, not getting those tiny follicles
are armor, tentacles sensing danger, your
fuzz Now I lion you into the world

Lungs, I've learned you house grief;
I apologize for what I did & didn't
cause, a heavy load these last years—
now I offer the tenderness of air

Dear brow, plucked & waxed &
scrunched, when all you ever wanted
was a curve, a broadcast, an open view
I promise the grace of the crease today

Arms, my wings, my friends, my journey
women, I think we understand each other—
carrying water buckets, leaflets &
daughters, my cradle, my ambassadors

Ok heart, for you I'll delve into cliché—
sorry I race when I should be listening,
sorry for amnesia & neglecting to consult;
thank you for outliving your enemies

For the flaps & harmless red spots
growing like volunteers in my field, for the un-
admired, the hidden, the folds my modesty
chooses to protect, I will try to love you

My father

wanted to divine
water with a stick on a hill
in Vermont Tap a tree
for syrup He built a cabin,
loved fresh-sliced pink bark,
strong black steaming coffee,
waxing skis with his hands
He wrote on a lined pad with
pencil & refused to wear
a tie or stand for the flag

I walked a pine-needle path
at night to get to his cedar
outhouse, rinsed my hands
in a white ceramic bowl
At 12 he gave up God but
continued to fast on Yom
Kippur, eat bitter herbs at
Seder At 75 he rode his bike
from Manhattan to Camel's
Hump Waning

on a sofa in his West Village
walkup, body betrayed at 83,
he asked me: *what do you mean*
when you say spiritual?
I looked to the skylight,
then at my father's drawn, long,
intelligent face, the darkly lit
eyes we shared, lifted my shoulders:
Maybe it's what we don't know

Becoming

This morning on my jog to & beside the blue silver Hudson licking the piers
I walked as a teen, the river my dad loved, now greened & spotted with kick

boxers, personal trainers & many sized dogs—I audibly thank each worker
I pass in orange or blue coveralls—some I imagine in the W.E.P

just released from a place with iron bars, some with hard hat, dust rolling
through their eyes, some guiding schoolchildren through the dangerous traffic

of the 21st century I smile, say hello, risking no response, risking seeming
ridiculous, because after 60 I can Each exchange opens space in my body,

each on this cloudy morning smiles back, some small in the mouth's corners,
some bigger stretching the face Each says *you're welcome* This is not to boast

my giddy gratitude at legs working & having the time to move through these
streets at 7 a.m. in the rusty air, but to say out loud on this page that let's face it,

yesterday I made at least five significant mistakes & can simply acknowledge
a stranger working on my behalf in a city whose pain wraps around itself

so tight it cuts off blood flow, too exhausted & perpetual to just burst
open like water from a hydrant—or unravel altogether It takes nothing

from me, & today, after the river, filled by the simplest of human nods, walking back
on Bedford or Carmine, I finally once again after years turn down Leroy Street, where

my brother dead from shame lived in his twenties I stand, planted on the sidewalk,
surrounded by strangers & ghosts, walk to Murray's cheese shop, moved from Cornelia,

which had been Rocco's, where he worked when out of work I order coffee at the newish
Amy's at Bleecker, take inventory, fall in love with each artwork on the walls, want to buy

Amy's t-shirt & coffee cup, to make this my new special place, to bring my daughters
& husband here I stand in the fragile, vast space between the dead & the living,

Gratitude

This morning the sun souses
& shimmers through trees swaying

in an arc over a road I've never before
noticed called Millstone: two syllables,

accrued weight Soon leaves
will flame & fall to the ground like prayer

reminding me why I keep vigil at the town
square, draft statements, help build a school

This morning after the first sip of *Native Thunder*
coffee roasted by a neighbor, while picking up last

night's cups stuffed with crumpled tissue, I'm not
annoyed about the mess but grateful the messers are

here walking through the house in underwear &
unbrushed endless hair—they are my life as is

the light seducing the trees My daughters, blinking
like stars dropped onto earth, appear on this

summer morning, & first Johnny Cash
then Chucho Valdés ripples through the house

We plan what we will cook for dinner; green beans
their father grew spill out of baskets and bowls

The Last Letter

Zebra, your stripes make me gag—
never that clear, black or white

Liar, zebra—give me gray where I can stay—mud, mess,
mush (oh I've strayed back to *m*)

Or no—I change my mind, I do want clear—
a line, a bite, a choice, zig or zag

Or zero Give me blessed zero. Beginning, egg, oh zero,
encircle me, break open too, no corners, only *z z z z*
eternity

Blessed be what stays Give me what stays The z's,
some sleep Please Sibling? (no, that's *s*)

Return to z Zone LifeZone StartZone, endZone, noZone,
oZone, loveZone, breathZone, how to name a zillion

sadnesses leading to your deathZone?
I can't breathe in this zone, dead brother, please grant me joyZone

Or just some peaceZone   Take me back to A
Aware A in wave Or pray Alive Aaaah Stay

Once upon A

Notes

"the body i write for" is for Cheryl Boyce-Taylor, the title from a prompt in her Zuihitsu workshop.

"Horses, still" is after Michael McGriff's "Why I Am Obsessed with Horses."

In "Dad, Pete & Obama," Pete refers to Pete Seeger and Toshi to his wife, Toshi Seeger. June refers to June Jordan.

"Block Island Tanka Morning" is after Muriel Rukeyser.

"Begin again" is after Grace Paley.

"not there" was written following the 2010 earthquake in Haiti.

In "Coffee," Grace refers to Grace Paley.

"Text message from best friend in Buffalo" is for Alexis De Veaux—her words, found poem.

In "Father Tanka," "Spring and Fall: To a Young Child" is a poem by Gerard Manley Hopkins.

"Where" is for Suheir Hammad.

"Praise Song for a Farmer" is in memory of Bud (Honey), my stepfather. *Duck blind* is a covered area where hunters sit or crouch near water where the ducks are. *Blues* are blue fish.

"Breasts & Interrogation" refers to the Palestinian village of Lyd.

"We Have Been Here a Long Time" is for Jon.

In "Becoming," W.E.P. refers to the Work Experience Program.

"Gratitude" is for Ella and Jaja.

Thank You

Is not enough. Not at all.

Ella, Jaja. Everything. You both amaze me, fill me with gratitude, love, hope. Make me laugh, remind me humility. Inspire me. Every day. And that would be enough.

Jon, beloved. All the years, how we've stayed, built, deepening. Every early draft. Your love of life most of all.

Tinka, the way you show up, your steadfast faith in me, your grit, leadership, vibrancy, courage.

Sooz and Jen, sisters. Always. So many ways.

Sooz, you listened gracefully and lovingly to the first drafts of many of *The Lost Brother Alphabet* poems when we were at Hedgebrook together. That was enormous. Jen, you and Chris hosted me, changed your plans to attend the performance in Santa Monica.
And mostly, all the ways …

Alexis. Best friend, poet and outlaw sister, how we be, how we grow. Beyond words.

The whole family. Families. As we continue. Stumble. Change. Keep trying. Learning.

I won't name you all, poem hearts, friends, colleagues, guides, inspirers … so forgive me… and you know who you are; the list gorgeously grows. How deeply fortunate I am to have somehow journeyed with you, touched, been touched by you, learned from you. Sonia Sanchez. Valerie Maynard. Yesenia Montilla. Cheryl Boyce-Taylor. Gale P. Jackson. Gwendolen Hardwick. Sandra Garcia Betancourt. Caits Meissner. Ellen Hagan. Lisa Wujnovich. LeConté Dill. Mihaela Moscaliuc. Samantha Thornhill. Elana Bell. Jessica Leighton. Melissa Tuckey. Elisa Biagini. Nathalie Handal. Suheir Hammad. JP Howard. EJ Antonio. Adonis Volanakis. Christina Olivares. Alexis Pauline Gumbs. Deborah Kapchan. Julia Sangodare Wallace. Jesse Pasca. Carole Alexis. Jean Pierre. Rev. Osageyfo Uhuru Sekou. Omo Moses and family. Marta Moreno Vega. Margaret Ratner. Sarah and Emily Kunstler. Michael Waters. Sarah Browning. E. Ethelbert Miller. Mbachi Kumwenda. Naimah Holmes. Grace Aneiza Ali. Tohanash Tarrant. Adam Horowitz. Susan Sherman. Karen Meyer. Maaza Mengiste. Harriet Barlow. Deborah Willis. Tina

Chang. Naomi Shihab Nye. Dipti Desai. Stephen Duncombe. Marlene Ramirez-Cancio. Leslie Cagan. Blanche Wiesen Cook. Clare Coss. Susan L. Taylor. Tiyé Giraud. Rev. Kimberly Quinn Johnson. Digna Sanchez. Darlene Charneco. Edwidge Danticat. Tina Orlandini. Lynne McEniry. Mark Read. Pamela Tinnen. Margaretha Haughwout. Belvie Rooks. Noliwe Rooks. Bill Gaskins. Laura Flanders. Eve Ensler. Terry Winchell. Rosalba Rolon. Alvan Colon Lespier. Scott Aviles Barton. Kyla Searle—you came to my home and helped me throw things away! Refilwe Nkomo, how better to finally visit South Africa than invited by you, at/with Lalela, *a place of listening*. Ginger Gillespie. Gwen McKinney. Sokari Ekine. Billie Jean Young. Allyson Pimental, Ava Noguera, Pedro Noguera. Susan Meiselas. Suchi Branfman for all the years—moving and making/making things happen, for taking the suite, *The Lost Brother Alphabet*, into your choreographic body.

Leah Natasha Thomas, you generously, brilliantly brought "To Kneel" to life with almost no resources and little time. Thanks for the support of the NYU Tisch Dean's Faculty Grant, PEN America, Bowery Poetry, The Root, Anne Hess and Craig Kaplan, Catherine and Rony Shimony, Toni Ross. To Alexis De Veaux, Anna Deavere Smith, Naomi Shihab Nye, Sandra Garcia Betancourt, Walter Mosley, Anooj Bhandari, E. Ethelbert Miller, Danny Glover, Kathleen Chalfant, Oskar Eustis, for bringing your voices to "Who Will Kneel For You." Mariah McClain. Melissa Murray.

Flora Brandl and Joanna Ruth Evans. You know I couldn't have done this work without your, each of your, meticulous, generous, brilliant assistance. Thank you for your patience.

Amy, Ginny, Francesca, Bernadette. You held me through the great tangle.

Thank you for an early deeply helpful read, Michael Waters, and for suggesting two books might be one. Thank you endlessly, Anne Marie Macari and Alicia Ostriker, for reading the manuscript, your essential generous eyes and ears, and for sharing your words, for teaching me, still. Ross Gay, thank you each day for opening poetic, intertwining paths, such robust generosity, coming to my classes, and writing on my behalf. Aracelis Girmay for your exquisite way of reading and writing your own words in conversation with the ones I offer, with poignant care. For showing me the lives of poems. And more.

Teachers and students from my time at the Drew University MFA Program in Poetry and Poetry in Translation.

Abundance of beloveds, sometimes called students and alumni, you know who you are—I thank you for trusting me, learning with me, teaching me, re-making the world, giving me hope every day. Faculty and staff of the Department of Art & Public Policy at NYU, Tisch School of the Arts, for your support, your patience, your work—the way you model arts/politics.

Blue Mountain Center. Hedgebrook. For the time, beauty, space, food, camaraderie, to think, write, imagine, get stuck, walk, run. Hobart Festival of Women Writers, Cheryl and Breena Clarke. Herstory. For the beauty of and welcome to La Pietra at a time when I needed that, thank you, amazing Ellyn Toscano.

First poem teachers: Jean Valentine, and in memoriam, Galway Kinnell. Jane Cooper. Cynthia Macdonald.

To KBL for helping me see, trust, accept (more!).

In memory: June Jordan. Ingrid Washinawatok. Kamal Boullata. Safiya Henderson Holmes. Donald Walter Woods. Sekou Sundiata. John Trudell. Elizabeth Thunderbird Haile. Grace Paley. Grace Lee Boggs. Melanie Kaye Kantrowitz. Randy Martin. Bud (Honey) Topping. Rosa Bromberg. Monroe Engel. Henrietta and Henry Engel. Lina and Red Derecktor.

Jasper, Gavin, Ruby, Elizabeth, who most intimately loved and lost your father and husband (my brother)—I hope you feel the poems as love. They are only my story, or part of it. Sonya, I honor the deep love and devotion you shared with my father so many years.

Horse. Tree. Sea.

Roberto Garcia, thank you for the gorgeous vision and energy to build a poetic community called Get Fresh Books Publishing. Darla Himeles, Ann Hagerty Davenport, Victoria Robinson, the whole team. Thank you enormously.

Philippe Cheng, thank you for the gift of your eye. What you see and make and share. For the cover of this book. I'm deeply honored and moved by your sense of beauty and your grace.

The list is incomplete and inadequate. I do nothing alone. Thank you.

Acknowledgments

I gratefully acknowledge these publications in which the following poems, or versions of them, were first published or will appear:

Poet Lore
"Begin again," "My daughter's convinced," "Volunteer," "Return," "Since We're Talking About Love"

Poetry—special issue on Eco Justice and *What Saves Us: Poems of Empathy and Outrage in the Age of Trump*
"Now I Pray"

Women's Voices for Change
"Amends to Parts of the Body"

5 A.M.
"Block Island Tanka Morning," "Coffee"

Vandal
"Where," "Breasts & Interrogation"

Foreign Policy in Focus
"Where"

The Wide Shore
"A"

Adanna
"Dad, Pete & Obama"

On the Issues
"Horse & Fire Dream"

Split This Rock Blog
"Dad, Pete & Obama"

Beloit Poetry Journal/Split This Rock Chapbook 2012
"Gratitude"

Ghost Fishing, An Eco-Justice Poetry Anthology
"Return," "Now I Pray"

The East Hampton Star and *Beloit Poetry Journal*
"Gratitude"

Long Island Sounds: 2019
"the body i write for"

Portside
"To Kneel"

About the Poet

Kathy Engel is a poet, essayist, educator and cultural worker who, over the last 40 years, has worked in many of the social justice, peace, and human rights movements in the U.S. and in solidarity with those around the world. She has co-founded and led organizations including the women's human rights group, *MADRE.org*, consulted with campaigns, and curated cultural political events. She teaches in the Department of Art & Public Policy, Tisch School of the Arts, NYU. Her books include *Banish the Tentative*, a chapbook (Wingding & Honey Publications, 1989); *Ruth's Skirts* (IKON, 2007); *The Kitchen*, in collaboration with artist German Perez (Yaboa Press, 2011); and *We Begin Here: Poems for Palestine and Lebanon* (Interlink Books, 2007). The video work *Whowillkneel4you?* (2018) appears on *The Root*. Kathy lives with her partner, Jonathan Snow, in Sagaponack, NY and also in NYC for teaching. kathyengelpoet.com.

www.ingramcontent.com/pod-product-compliance
Lightning Source LLC
Chambersburg PA
CBHW081157070526
44583CB00021B/2876